**30 Days to Believing
What God Says About You**

BIGGER
faith

DR. BRUCE BECKER

Published by Straight Talk Books
P.O. Box 301, Milwaukee, WI 53201
800.661.3311 • timeofgrace.org

Printed in the United States of America
ISBN: 978-1-949488-70-8

Introduction

Hey, friend, how big is your faith?

I know this is an intensely personal question, but it's an important one. So do you have a big faith, a small faith, or one that is somewhere in between? Or perhaps you aren't even sure how to answer the question.

Let's look at this from another perspective. Have you ever met a fellow Christian who wants a smaller faith than the one they currently have? I haven't. I've never met a Christian who desires a smaller faith. The Christians I know all seem to want a bigger faith, a stronger faith. Personally, I want a bigger faith. I want a rock-solid, never-wavering, ever-maturing trust in Jesus and his promises.

When Jesus walked this earth with his disciples, he admonished them on five different occasions for having *little* faith. However, Jesus also encountered two people whom he described as having *great* faith, one a man and one a woman. And do you know what they had in common? They weren't Jews. They were both Gentiles, a term used to describe non-Jews in the ancient world. The man was a Roman soldier. The woman was a Canaanite living in the region of Tyre and Sidon, northwest of the land of Israel.

Let's take a look at the two people whom Jesus said had *great* faith and see what else they had in common. First, the centurion:

> **When Jesus had entered Capernaum, a centurion came to him, asking for help. "Lord," he said, "my servant lies at home paralyzed, suffering terribly."**
>
> **Jesus said to him, "Shall I come and heal him?"**
>
> **The centurion replied, "Lord, I do not deserve to have you come under my roof. But just say the word, and my servant will be healed. For I myself am a man under authority, with soldiers under me. I tell this one, 'Go,' and he goes; and that one, 'Come,' and he comes. I say to**

my servant, 'Do this,' and he does it."

When Jesus heard this, he was amazed and said to those following him, "Truly I tell you, I have not found anyone in Israel with such great faith."

Then Jesus said to the centurion, "Go! Let it be done just as you believed it would." And his servant was healed at that moment. (Matthew 8:5-10,13)

One day, early in his three-year ministry, Jesus entered the town of Capernaum. Capernaum was a fishing village located on the north shore of the Sea of Galilee. Capernaum was also the hometown of one of Jesus' closest disciples, Simon Peter. He lived there with his wife and mother-in-law.

Upon entering the town of Capernaum, a Roman centurion approached Jesus with a request. He asked Jesus for help for his servant who was paralyzed and suffering. When Jesus asked if he should come to the centurion's home and heal the man, the centurion humbly indicated that he wasn't worthy to have Jesus come to his house. Besides, there was no need for it. "Just say the word, and my servant will be healed." That's faith in the power of Jesus!

The centurion approached Jesus with a request, not for himself but for his servant, who was suffering terribly. He was humble in his request yet confident in Jesus' power to heal his servant without even being in the same room as his servant. The centurion was a man of great faith. So Jesus healed the centurion's servant on the spot.

Second, the Canaanite woman:

Leaving that place, Jesus withdrew to the region of Tyre and Sidon. A Canaanite woman from that vicinity came to him, crying out, "Lord, Son of David, have mercy on me! My daughter is demon-possessed and suffering terribly."

Jesus did not answer a word. So his disciples came to him and urged him, "Send her away, for she keeps crying out after us."

He answered, "I was sent only to the lost sheep of Israel."

The woman came and knelt before him. "Lord, help me!" she said.

He replied, "It is not right to take the children's bread and toss it to the dogs."

"Yes it is, Lord," she said. "Even the dogs eat the crumbs that fall from their master's table."

Then Jesus said to her, "Woman, you have great faith! Your request is granted." And her daughter was healed at that moment. (Matthew 15:21–28)

The Canaanite woman also approached Jesus with a request for another person, her daughter. Her daughter was demon possessed and suffering terribly. Jesus initially ignored her, even though she kept crying out. Her persistent cries began to annoy the disciples, who asked Jesus to send her away. Ignoring someone in need wasn't Jesus' normal response. And then the words that Jesus spoke seem strange to us and even insulting to the woman.

To understand Jesus' encounter with the Canaanite woman, we need to keep in mind what the apostle Paul wrote in Romans chapter 1: **"I am not ashamed of the gospel, because it is the power of God that brings salvation to everyone who believes: first to the Jew, then to the Gentile** (Romans 1:16). Salvation is for *everyone* who believes, but there is an order of priority—Jews first, then Gentiles.

Now there are numerous reasons for "Jews first." For example, the Jews were God's Old Testament chosen people. They were the guardians of the Old Testament Scriptures. Jesus was born a Jew to save the Jews as the Christ, the promised Messiah. Even the salvation of Gentiles originated with the Lord's relationship with the Jews.

Back to what Jesus said. Jesus' personal ministry was indeed limited to the land of Israel even though he came to save the world. The "children" Jesus spoke about were the Jews, and the "bread" were the blessings of God in whatever form those blessings took. Jesus said, "It is not right to take the children's bread and toss it to the dogs."

It's interesting to note that the word Jesus used, translated as "dog," means a little lapdog, one that a child would have as a pet, one that would live with a family in their home.

We might think that after hearing what Jesus said, the woman would have felt rebuffed, insulted, and discouraged. But she wasn't. She saw an opening to ask again for Jesus' help. How she responded revealed her *great* faith.

The woman responded with humility, wisdom, and faith: "'Yes it is, Lord,' she said. 'Even the dogs eat the crumbs that fall from their master's table.'" What the woman said can be understood in one of two ways. The first way is that she was agreeing with Jesus but then went on to make a further point about the puppy dogs eating crumbs that fell from the table. The second way is that she actually disagreed with Jesus. Jesus had said, "It is not right to take the children's bread and toss it to the dogs." She responded, "Yes, it is (right), Lord, to take the children's bread and toss it to the dogs." The original biblical text allows for either understanding of the woman's words.

Either way, the woman's point was clear. What she was asking for, as a Gentile woman, was to have some of the scraps of blessing be given to her daughter. We all know that food falls from a table accidently, or it is dropped intentionally by someone sitting at the table. (I've seen my grandchildren do this very thing, usually with a sly smirk on their faces.) The woman asked Jesus for a few crumbs of blessing for her Gentile daughter.

In response to the woman's words, Jesus commended her for her great faith and healed her daughter at that very moment. Note the similarities between the Roman centurion and the Canaanite woman—1. humility, 2. asking for help for someone else, 3. confident trust in Jesus' willingness and power to heal (both individuals were healed immediately), 4. BOTH the Roman centurion and Canaanite woman were recognized by Jesus for having *great* faith.

You and I may never have a great faith like the Roman centurion or the Canaanite woman, but wouldn't you like to have a bigger faith? You know, a faith that trusts more, a faith that approaches God with greater humility, a faith that is unwavering, and a faith that responds confidently to any of life's struggles with a bold shout-out: "God's got this!"

So what's standing in the way of you and me getting a bigger faith? It seems to me there are two main obstacles to a bigger faith. One obstacle is the lies we believe. The other is the truth that we don't believe. And I'm talking here about GOD's TRUTH.

The lies that we believe have their source in what we might call an "unholy trio," three enemies that put obstacles in our path to a bigger faith.

The Enemies

Enemy #1 is Satan. During an encounter with the religious leaders of Israel, Jesus called Satan the father of lies because he has been lying from the beginning. We recall his tactics in the Garden of Eden with Adam and Eve. Satan suggested to Eve that she eat from the tree of the knowledge of good and evil (the only tree God said not to eat from). Satan conned Eve with two back-to-back lies. The first lie was totally untrue. The second one was a half-lie. Satan promised Eve, **"You will not certainly die"** and **"You will be like God, knowing good and evil"** (Genesis 3:4,5). Eve believed the lies, as did her husband, Adam, and in doing so broke the perfect faith trust between God and the first couple.

Enemy #2 is the culture in which we live. "Culture" refers to the customary beliefs, social norms, and characteristics of everyday life that are shared by people in a specific space and time. Although there are positives in our culture, not everything about culture aligns with God's truth. It's because there are people in our culture who tell lies.

Let's be honest. There are people in our culture who tell lies about when life begins and who has the right to end life. Other people tell lies about sexual freedom and gender fluidity. There are lies and half-truths about race and social justice with the claim that there is only one way to approach these issues. And the list goes on, cutting across all aspects of our culture. Too often, people in our culture make truth a lie and a lie the truth. When we believe any of the lies that our culture holds up as truth, we prevent ourselves from experiencing a bigger faith.

Then there is enemy #3. This enemy lives within us. It shows up in the lies we tell ourselves. It can be lies involving our thoughts or our feelings. The truth is that what we think about ourselves isn't always true. What we feel about ourselves isn't always true either. The lies we tell ourselves often have to do with what gives us value, respect, or success.

Believing the lies, no matter what the source, is one obstacle to gaining a bigger faith. The other obstacle is not believing the truth, God's truth. Here is an important point. The way to overcome the first obstacle, the lies, is to focus on overcoming the second obstacle, not believing God's truth. When we know God's truth, we won't be as tempted to believe the lies of Satan, our culture, or the lies we tell ourselves.

God's truth is revealed to us in the Bible. The Bible is an amazing book on many different levels. It was written over a period of 1,600 years by dozens of different authors. The Bible contains more than 700,000 words found in 66 individual historical books, prophecies, songs, or letters. There are 39 books in the Old Testament and 27 in the New Testament.

The main message of the Bible, a thread that runs from the beginning to the end, is that **"God so loved the world that he gave his one and only Son** [Jesus]**, that whoever believes in him shall not perish but have eternal life"** (John 3:16). God's Son left heaven to come to this earth to deal with the consequences of Adam and Eve believing Satan's lie in the Garden of Eden. The Bible's main message is God's message, God's truth. The Bible is the living and powerful Word of God!

The apostle Paul, in his letter to the Christians living in the Greek city of Thessalonica, explained what the Word of God is and what it does: **"And we also thank God continually because, when you received the word of God, which you heard from us, you accepted it not as a human word, but as it actually is, the word of God, which is indeed at work in you who believe"** (1 Thessalonians 2:13).

The Word of God, the message of God's love for people, is at work in the lives of those who believe.

The New Testament writer to the Hebrews also wrote: **"The word of God is alive and active. Sharper than any double-edged sword, it penetrates even to dividing soul and spirit, joints and marrow; it judges the thoughts and attitudes of the heart"** (4:12). The Bible is the living and powerful Word of God!

Do you know what one of the biggest lies Satan, our culture, and even ourselves want people to believe? It's the lie that the Bible really *isn't* the Word of God, that it's not trustworthy, and that it isn't totally accurate. But if the Bible isn't the Word

of God, then how can we be sure that God has secured eternal life for us with him in heaven? If the Bible isn't the Word of God, then our faith has nothing to rest upon. If the Bible isn't the Word of God, then our faith has no foundation and we are fools for believing it.

But the Bible is the living and powerful Word of God! But how can that be? How can the words of the Bible be God's Word when human beings authored it? The Bible explains that too.

Before Jesus ascended into heaven, he told his disciples about the Holy Spirit's role in their future: **"The Advocate, the Holy Spirit, whom the Father will send in my name, will teach you all things and will remind you of everything I said to you"** (John 14:26). The Holy Spirit would guide the authors of the books of the Bible as to what to write.

In his second letter, the apostle Peter spoke about the origin of the Bible, specifically prophecy: **"Prophecy never had its origin in the human will, but prophets, though human, spoke from God as they were carried along by the Holy Spirit"** (2 Peter 1:21). Prophets who shared a message with God's people were speaking for God himself. A prophet was the mouthpiece of God.

In his letter to Pastor Timothy, the apostle Paul also wrote about the Holy Spirit's role in the writing of the biblical text, as well as the power of the Word in people's lives: **"But as for you, continue in what you have learned and have become convinced of, because you know those from whom you learned it, and how from infancy you have known the Holy Scriptures, which are able to make you wise for salvation through faith in Christ Jesus. All Scripture is God-breathed and is useful for teaching, rebuking, correcting and training in righteousness, so that the servant of God may be thoroughly equipped for every good work"** (2 Timothy 3:14-17).

The phrase "God-breathed" points to the Holy Spirit's work of giving the biblical authors both the thoughts and the words they wrote. Bible scholars call this verbal inspiration.

Besides being God-breathed, the apostle tells about the value and blessing of God's Word. It is useful for *teaching*—teaching me God's truth. It is useful for *rebuking*—pointing out the lies in my life that show up in my thoughts, my feelings, and my

actions. It is useful for *correcting*—showing me what God's will actually is for my life. It is also useful for *training in righteousness*—training me to live as God's child.

In another of his letters, the apostle Paul put it this way: **"Faith comes from hearing the message, and the message is heard through the word about Christ"** (Romans 10:17). Do you see the connection here between God's Word and faith? We gain a bigger faith when we read or listen to the Word of God.

Finally, the apostle Peter addressed the two obstacles standing in the way of gaining a bigger faith:

> **"Therefore, dear friends, since you have been forewarned, be on your guard so that you may not be carried away by the error of the lawless and fall from your secure position. But grow** [literally "keep growing"] **in the grace and knowledge of our Lord and Savior Jesus Christ. To him be glory both now and forever! Amen."** (2 Peter 3:17,18)

So what does this mean for those of us who want a bigger faith? To gain a bigger faith, we need to stop believing the lies and fix our thoughts on the central message of the Bible.

Now this may sound simple and straightforward, but it is incredibly challenging. The lies that we believe are real and often a real and tough struggle not to believe them. Sometimes we don't even recognize that we are believing a lie. And you and I can't just flip a switch and say, "I'm not going to believe that lie anymore" and think that's all it takes.

In reality, it's a daily struggle not to believe the lies. But when we focus on what God has to say in his Word, we bring him into our struggles. We bring his truth into our lies. That's a good thing. That's a helpful thing. We know that the Holy Spirit works through the Word to build our faith, our trust, and our confidence. Saying no to the lies and yes to God's truth happens day by day, one step at a time.

So let's fix our thoughts on Jesus!

Every day.

30 Days to a Bigger Faith

Are you ready to begin a 30-day journey to a bigger faith that believes what God says about you? You can do this by yourself, or you can invite a friend to join you so you can take the journey together.

On each of the 30 days, you will have the opportunity

- to learn about a lie that Christians often struggle with (not all Christians struggle with all 30 lies).

- to discern how much you struggle with the lie, whether it is *rarely, sometimes, often,* or *all the time.*

- to describe the circumstances when the lie shows up in your life (or if it isn't a lie you struggle with, you can describe how a friend or family member struggles with it).

- to read and ponder God's Word to learn how God's truth opposes the lie.

- to journal how you will fix your thoughts more on Jesus and form a new thought pattern.

- to journal how you will fight the lie and embrace God's truth.

- to write a prayer asking Jesus to help you fight the lie and embrace his truth.

My prayer for you is that this 30-day journey will help you gain a bigger faith. Fix your thoughts on Jesus!

Day One

The Lie
God doesn't love me.

I struggle with this lie . . .

| rarely | sometimes | often | all the time |

I feel like God doesn't love me when . . .

_____

_____

_____

_____

_____

_____

The Bible Says

This is how God showed his love among us: He sent his one and only Son into the world that we might live through him. This is love: not that we loved God, but that he loved us and sent his Son as an atoning sacrifice for our sins. . . . God is love. Whoever lives in love lives in God, and God in them. (1 John 4:9,10,16)

For I am convinced that neither death nor life, neither angels nor demons, neither the present nor the future, nor any powers, neither height nor depth, nor anything else in all creation, will be able to separate us from the love of God that is in Christ Jesus our Lord. (Romans 8:38,39)

God's Truth

God loves me because he is love. He loves me perfectly and unconditionally. Nothing can ever separate me from his love.

A New Thought Pattern

Based on God's truth, how can I be sure that God loves me even if I don't "feel" it?

_____

_____

_____

What will I do today to fix my thoughts more on Jesus and embrace God's truth?

_____

_____

_____

My Prayer

Dear Jesus,

_____

_____

_____

_____

_____

Day Two

The Lie
God won't forgive me for what I've done.

I struggle with this lie . . .

| rarely | sometimes | often | all the time |

I question my forgiveness when I . . .

_____

_____

_____

The Bible Says

As far as the east is from the west, so far has he removed our transgressions from us. (Psalm 103:12)

For I will forgive their wickedness and will remember their sins no more. (Jeremiah 31:34)

Who is a God like you, who pardons sin and forgives the transgression of the remnant of his inheritance? You do not stay angry forever but delight to show mercy. You will again have compassion on us; you will tread our sins underfoot and hurl all our iniquities into the depths of the sea. (Micah 7:18,19)

In him [Jesus] we have redemption through his blood, the forgiveness of sins, in accordance with the riches of God's grace. (Ephesians 1:7)

If we confess our sins, he is faithful and just and will forgive us our sins and purify us from all unrighteousness. (1 John 1:9)

God's Truth

God's grace is always greater than my sin. When Jesus was crucified, he endured God's punishment for every one of my sins. God forgives me completely because of Jesus and remembers my sin no more.

A New Thought Pattern

The beauty of grace is that no matter my sin, Jesus has taken it all away. Reminding myself of this, I can look at my past missteps and . . .

What will I do today to fix my thoughts more on Jesus and embrace God's truth?

My Prayer

Dear Jesus,

Day Three

The Lie
I don't have enough faith.

I struggle with this lie . . .

| rarely | sometimes | often | all the time |

I worry about this lie because . . .

_____

_____

_____

_____

The Bible Says

"Truly I tell you, if you have faith as small as a mustard seed, you can say to this mountain, 'Move from here to there,' and it will move. Nothing will be impossible for you." (Matthew 17:20)

The apostles said to the Lord, "Increase our faith!" He replied, "If you have faith as small as a mustard seed, you can say to this mulberry tree, 'Be uprooted and planted in the sea,' and it will obey you." (Luke 17:5,6)

For by the grace given me I say to every one of you: Do not think of yourself more highly than you ought, but rather think of yourself with sober judgment, in accordance with the faith God has distributed to each of you. (Romans 12:3)

My message and my preaching were not with wise and persuasive words, but with a demonstration of the Spirit's power, so that your faith might not rest on human wisdom, but on God's power. (1 Corinthians 2:4,5)

BIGGER *faith*

God's Truth

God has given me the faith I need and the source for increasing my faith.

A New Thought Pattern

Who are the people in my life who would encourage me to stay in God's Word more so the Holy Spirit can strengthen my faith?

_____

_____

_____

What will I do today to fix my thoughts more on Jesus and embrace God's truth?

_____

_____

_____

_____

My Prayer

Dear Jesus,

_____

_____

_____

_____

_____

Day Four

The Lie
God doesn't answer my prayers.

I struggle with this lie . . .

rarely   sometimes   often   all the time

I've been praying for these things, and it seems as if God isn't answering . . .

_____

_____

_____

The Bible Says

Then Jesus told his disciples a parable to show them that they should always pray and not give up. (Luke 18:1)

Be joyful in hope, patient in affliction, faithful in prayer. (Romans 12:12)

Now to him who is able to do immeasurably more than all we ask or imagine, according to his power that is at work within us, to him be glory in the church and in Christ Jesus throughout all generations, for ever and ever! Amen. (Ephesians 3:20,21)

Therefore confess your sins to each other and pray for each other so that you may be healed. The prayer of a righteous person is powerful and effective. (James 5:16)

For the eyes of the Lord are on the righteous and his ears are attentive to their prayer, but the face of the Lord is against those who do evil. (1 Peter 3:12)

BIGGER *faith*

God's Truth

God always hears my prayers. He will answer them according to his plans and timetable. I know God always wants what's best for me.

A New Thought Pattern

God promises to answer my prayers. In what ways could he be answering me right now for the prayers I mentioned earlier?

_____

_____

_____

What will I do today to fix my thoughts more on Jesus and embrace God's truth?

_____

_____

_____

_____

My Prayer

Dear Jesus,

_____

_____

_____

_____

Day Five

The Lie
I need to fear what might happen in the future.

I struggle with this lie . . .

○	○	○	○
rarely	*sometimes*	*often*	*all the time*

These are my fears about the future . . .

_____

_____

_____

_____

_____

The Bible Says

Even though I walk through the darkest valley, I will fear no evil, for you are with me. (Psalm 23:4)

"Are not two sparrows sold for a penny? Yet not one of them will fall to the ground outside your Father's care. And even the very hairs of your head are all numbered. So don't be afraid; you are worth more than many sparrows." (Matthew 10:29–31)

Keep your lives free from the love of money and be content with what you have, because God has said, "Never will I leave you; never will I forsake you." So we say with confidence, "The Lord is my helper; I will not be afraid. What can mere mortals do to me?" (Hebrews 13:5,6)

God's Truth

I have nothing to fear. God holds the future in his hands. God's got this!

A New Thought Pattern

When I worry about the future, how can I reframe those worries into confidence based on God's truth for me?

_____

_____

_____

What will I do today to fix my thoughts more on Jesus and embrace God's truth?

_____

_____

_____

My Prayer

Dear Jesus,

_____

_____

_____

_____

_____

Day Six

The Lie
I should always follow my heart.

I struggle with this lie . . .

rarely   sometimes   often   all the time

I follow my heart in my life when . . .

_____

_____

_____

_____

The Bible Says

The heart is deceitful above all things and beyond cure. Who can understand it? (Jeremiah 17:9)

"For out of the heart come evil thoughts—murder, adultery, sexual immorality, theft, false testimony, slander." (Matthew 15:19)

"For where your treasure is, there your heart will be also." (Luke 12:34)

Take delight in the Lord, and he will give you the desires of your heart. (Psalm 37:4)

Trust in the Lord with all your heart and lean not on your own understanding; in all your ways submit to him, and he will make your paths straight. (Proverbs 3:5,6)

Above all else, guard your heart, for everything you do flows from it. (Proverbs 4:23)

God's Truth

Since my heart can be either good or evil, I will follow my heart only when it aligns with God's heart.

A New Thought Pattern

Following my heart is God-pleasing when . . .

_____

_____

_____

Following my heart is NOT God-pleasing when . . .

_____

_____

_____

What will I do today to fix my thoughts more on Jesus and embrace God's truth?

_____

_____

_____

My Prayer

Dear Jesus,

_____

_____

_____

_____

Day Seven

The Lie
I lack what I really need in my life.

I struggle with this lie . . .

○——————————○——————————○——————————○

rarely   sometimes   often   all the time

I've noticed this creeping in when I think about . . .

_____

_____

_____

_____

The Bible Says

The eyes of all look to you, and you give them their food at the proper time. You open your hand and satisfy the desires of every living thing. (Psalm 145:15,16)

"So do not worry, saying, 'What shall we eat?' or 'What shall we drink?' or 'What shall we wear?' For the pagans run after all these things, and your heavenly Father knows that you need them. But seek first his kingdom and his righteousness, and all these things will be given to you as well." (Matthew 6:31-33)

And now, brothers and sisters, we want you to know about the grace that God has given the Macedonian churches. In the midst of a very severe trial, their overflowing joy and their extreme poverty welled up in rich generosity. (2 Corinthians 8:1,2)

And my God will meet all your needs according to the riches of his glory in Christ Jesus. To our God and Father be glory for ever and ever. Amen. (Philippians 4:19,20)

God's Truth

God has given me everything I need.

A New Thought Pattern

My list of needs vs. wants:

_____

_____

_____

_____

What will I do today to fix my thoughts more on Jesus and embrace God's truth?

_____

_____

_____

_____

My Prayer

Dear Jesus,

_____

_____

_____

_____

_____

Day Eight

The Lie
I can face life's challenges on my own.

I struggle with this lie . . .

rarely   sometimes   often   all the time

I tend to think I can take on challenges on my own when . . .

The Bible Says

Though one may be overpowered, two can defend themselves. A cord of three strands is not quickly broken. (Ecclesiastes 4:12)

I rejoiced greatly in the Lord that at last you renewed your concern for me. Indeed, you were concerned, but you had no opportunity to show it. I am not saying this because I am in need, for I have learned to be content whatever the circumstances. I know what it is to be in need, and I know what it is to have plenty. I have learned the secret of being content in any and every situation, whether well fed or hungry, whether living in plenty or in want. I can do all this through him who gives me strength. (Philippians 4:10-13)

Humble yourselves, therefore, under God's mighty hand, that he may lift you up in due time. Cast all your anxiety on him because he cares for you. (1 Peter 5:6,7)

God's Truth

I can better face life's challenges when I have the strength given to me by Jesus.

A New Thought Pattern

I need God, and I need other people when I'm struggling with challenges. Which people in my life would be good to go to for help?

What will I do today to fix my thoughts more on Jesus and embrace God's truth?

My Prayer

Dear Jesus,

Day Nine

The Lie
It is impossible to resist temptation.

I struggle with this lie . . .

| rarely | sometimes | often | all the time |

These particular temptations are hard for me to resist . . .

_____

_____

_____

The Bible Says

So, if you think you are standing firm, be careful that you don't fall! No temptation has overtaken you except what is common to mankind. And God is faithful; he will not let you be tempted beyond what you can bear. But when you are tempted, he will also provide a way out so that you can endure it. (1 Corinthians 10:12,13)

When tempted, no one should say, "God is tempting me." For God cannot be tempted by evil, nor does he tempt anyone; but each person is tempted when they are dragged away by their own evil desire and enticed. Then, after desire has conceived, it gives birth to sin; and sin, when it is full-grown, gives birth to death. (James 1:13-15)

So I say, walk by the Spirit, and you will not gratify the desires of the flesh. For the flesh desires what is contrary to the Spirit, and the Spirit what is contrary to the flesh. They are in conflict with each other, so that you are not to do whatever you want. But if you are led by the Spirit, you are not under the law. (Galatians 5:16-18)

God's Truth

I am able to resist temptation when I live by the Spirit.

A New Thought Pattern

When I'm feeling tempted, what can I remember about my Savior Jesus and the temptations he encountered on earth?

_____

_____

_____

Jesus understands my temptations. What does that mean for me?

_____

_____

_____

What will I do today to fix my thoughts more on Jesus and embrace God's truth?

_____

_____

_____

My Prayer

Dear Jesus,

_____

_____

_____

_____

Day Ten

The Lie
*I need to have people like/love me
in order to have value in my life.*

I struggle with this lie . . .

rarely	sometimes	often	all the time

I feel like I have no value when . . .

_____

_____

_____

_____

The Bible Says

For you created my inmost being; you knit me together in my mother's womb. I praise you because I am fearfully and wonderfully made; your works are wonderful, I know that full well. My frame was not hidden from you when I was made in the secret place, when I was woven together in the depths of the earth. Your eyes saw my unformed body; all the days ordained for me were written in your book before one of them came to be. How precious to me are your thoughts, God! How vast is the sum of them! Were I to count them, they would outnumber the grains of sand. (Psalm 139:13-18)

And we know that in all things God works for the good of those who love him, who have been called according to his purpose. (Romans 8:28)

But you are a chosen people, a royal priesthood, a holy nation, God's special possession, that you may declare the praises of him who called you out of darkness into his wonderful light. (1 Peter 2:9)

God's Truth

My value comes from the God who created me and his Son, who saved me.

A New Thought Pattern

What are some of the names that God calls me in the Bible that show me my value:

....

....

....

....

What will I do today to fix my thoughts more on Jesus and embrace God's truth?

....

....

....

....

My Prayer

Dear Jesus,

....

....

....

....

....

Day Eleven

The Lie
God can't use a person like me.

I struggle with this lie . . .

          ○   ○   ○   ○

rarely   *sometimes*   *often*   *all the time*

I believe this lie when . . .

_____

_____

_____

The Bible Says

But Moses said to God, "Who am I that I should go to Pharaoh and bring the Israelites out of Egypt?" And God said, "I will be with you. And this will be the sign to you that it is I who have sent you: When you have brought the people out of Egypt, you will worship God on this mountain." (Exodus 3:11,12)

"Pardon me, my lord," Gideon replied, "but how can I save Israel? My clan is the weakest in Manasseh, and I am the least in my family." The Lord answered, "I will be with you, and you will strike down all the Midianites, leaving none alive." (Judges 6:15,16)

Brothers and sisters, think of what you were when you were called. Not many of you were wise by human standards; not many were influential; not many were of noble birth. But God chose the foolish things of the world to shame the wise; God chose the weak things of the world to shame the strong. God chose the lowly things of this world and the despised things— and the things that are not—to nullify the things that are. (1 Corinthians 1:26-28)

God's Truth

God can use me because I belong to him and he is with me.

A New Thought Pattern

Instead of thinking of ways that God can't use me, here is a list of areas where I could serve others in my church, at home, or at work:

_____

_____

_____

What will I do today to fix my thoughts more on Jesus and embrace God's truth?

_____

_____

_____

My Prayer

Dear Jesus,

_____

_____

_____

_____

_____

Day Twelve

The Lie
*God's expectations for how I should
live my life seem unreasonable.*

I struggle with this lie . . .

rarely   sometimes   often   all the time

God's expectations don't seem fair when . . .

_____

_____

_____

_____

The Bible Says

The law of the Lᴏʀᴅ is perfect, refreshing the soul. The statutes of the Lᴏʀᴅ are trustworthy, making wise the simple. (Psalm 19:7)

Trust in the Lᴏʀᴅ with all your heart and lean not on your own understanding; in all your ways submit to him, and he will make your paths straight. Do not be wise in your own eyes." (Proverbs 3:5–7)

And we know that in all things God works for the good of those who love him, who have been called according to his purpose. (Romans 8:28)

Everyone who believes that Jesus is the Christ is born of God, and everyone who loves the father loves his child as well. This is how we know that we love the children of God: by loving God and carrying out his commands. In fact, this is love for God: to keep his commands. And his commands are not burdensome, for everyone born of God overcomes the world. (1 John 5:1–4)

God's Truth

God's ways are always best for me and will result in blessings for my life.

A New Thought Pattern

Instead of thinking that I know best, how has God already showed me that he loves me and has a plan for me?

_____

_____

_____

What will I do today to fix my thoughts more on Jesus and embrace God's truth?

_____

_____

_____

My Prayer

Dear Jesus,

_____

_____

_____

_____

_____

_____

Day Thirteen

The Lie
I need to be like that other person.

I struggle with this lie . . .

   rarely   sometimes   often   *all the time*

Sometimes I compare myself to other people when . . .

_____

_____

_____

_____

The Bible Says

For you created my inmost being; you knit me together in my mother's womb. I praise you because I am fearfully and wonderfully made; your works are wonderful, I know that full well. (Psalm 139:13,14)

A heart at peace gives life to the body, but envy rots the bones. (Proverbs 14:30)

And I saw that all toil and all achievement spring from one person's envy of another. This too is meaningless, a chasing after the wind. (Ecclesiastes 4:4)

The acts of the flesh are obvious: sexual immorality . . . and envy. (Galatians 5:19,21)

Love is patient, love is kind. It does not envy, it does not boast, it is not proud. (1 Corinthians 13:4)

God's Truth

God made me as an individual with my own abilities and spiritual gifts so that I don't have any reason to be envious of others.

A New Thought Pattern

What characteristics and abilities make me God's unique child?

_____

_____

_____

_____

What will I do today to fix my thoughts more on Jesus and embrace God's truth?

_____

_____

_____

_____

My Prayer

Dear Jesus,

_____

_____

_____

_____

_____

BIGGER *faith*

Day Fourteen

The Lie
I can't let others see my
vulnerabilities and weaknesses.

I struggle with this lie . . .

rarely   sometimes   often   all the time

I'm not super comfortable letting others see my flaws when . . .

_____

_____

_____

_____

_____

_____

The Bible Says

But we have this treasure in jars of clay to show that this all-surpassing power is from God and not from us. (2 Corinthians 4:7)

"My grace is sufficient for you, for my power is made perfect in weakness." Therefore I will boast all the more gladly about my weaknesses, so that Christ's power may rest on me. That is why, for Christ's sake, I delight in weaknesses, in insults, in hardships, in persecutions, in difficulties. For when I am weak, then I am strong. (2 Corinthians 12:9,10)

Carry each other's burdens, and in this way you will fulfill the law of Christ. (Galatians 6:2)

BIGGER *faith*

God's Truth

God wants me to share my vulnerabilities and weaknesses with my fellow Christians so they can help carry my burdens.

A New Thought Pattern

God has given me family and friends as a blessing. Who could I reach out to for help with my daily struggles?

What will I do today to fix my thoughts more on Jesus and embrace God's truth?

My Prayer

Dear Jesus,

Day Fifteen

The Lie
*As a Christian, I shouldn't have
to experience pain in my life.*

I struggle with this lie . . .

| rarely | sometimes | often | all the time |

I feel this way about pain when . . .

_____

_____

_____

_____

The Bible Says

The Lord is close to the brokenhearted and saves those who are crushed in spirit. The righteous person may have many troubles, but the Lord delivers him from them all. (Psalm 34:18,19)

He heals the brokenhearted and binds up their wounds. He determines the number of the stars and calls them each by name. Great is our Lord and mighty in power; his understanding has no limit. (Psalm 147:3-5)

I consider that our present sufferings are not worth comparing with the glory that will be revealed in us. (Romans 8:18)

In all this you greatly rejoice, though now for a little while you may have had to suffer grief in all kinds of trials. These have come so that the proven genuineness of your faith—of greater worth than gold, which perishes even though refined by fire—may result in praise, glory and honor when Jesus Christ is revealed. (1 Peter 1:6,7)

God's Truth

The pain I experience in my life as a Christian is temporary. My life with Christ in heaven will be perfectly pain-free.

A New Thought Pattern

Even if I'm in pain right now, what does God tell me about my pain and his presence?

What will I do today to fix my thoughts more on Jesus and embrace God's truth?

My Prayer

Dear Jesus,

Day Sixteen

The Lie
I should be afraid of dying.

I struggle with this lie . . .

rarely   sometimes   often   all the time

Recently, I've thought more about this when . . .

_____

_____

_____

_____

The Bible Says

"Do not let your hearts be troubled. You believe in God; believe also in me. My Father's house has many rooms; if that were not so, would I have told you that I am going there to prepare a place for you? And if I go and prepare a place for you, I will come back and take you to be with me that you also may be where I am." (John 14:1-3)

So will it be with the resurrection of the dead. The body that is sown is perishable, it is raised imperishable; it is sown in dishonor, it is raised in glory; it is sown in weakness, it is raised in power; it is sown a natural body, it is raised a spiritual body. If there is a natural body, there is also a spiritual body. (1 Corinthians 15:42-44)

And this is the testimony: God has given us eternal life, and this life is in his Son. Whoever has the Son has life. (1 John 5:11,12)

God's Truth

I already have eternal life as a follower of Jesus. Death is but the doorway to heaven to meet Jesus.

A New Thought Pattern

If I feel anxious about death, it can be really hard to break those thoughts even when I know God is with me. But instead of worrying about something I can't control, I'll remind myself that God is in control!

What will I do today to fix my thoughts more on Jesus and embrace God's truth?

My Prayer

Dear Jesus,

Day Seventeen

The Lie
No one loves me.

I struggle with this lie . . .

○	○	○	○
rarely	*sometimes*	*often*	*all the time*

Sometimes I feel unloved when . . .

_____

_____

_____

_____

The Bible Says

Your love, Lord, reaches to the heavens, your faithfulness to the skies. Your righteousness is like the highest mountains, your justice like the great deep. You, Lord, preserve both people and animals. How priceless is your unfailing love, O God! People take refuge in the shadow of your wings. (Psalm 36:5–7)

Who shall separate us from the love of Christ? Shall trouble or hardship or persecution or famine or nakedness or danger or sword? No, in all these things we are more than conquerors through him who loved us. For I am convinced that neither death nor life, neither angels nor demons, neither the present nor the future, nor any powers, neither height nor depth, nor anything else in all creation, will be able to separate us from the love of God that is in Christ Jesus our Lord. (Romans 8:35,37–39)

BIGGER *faith*

God's Truth

Even if there is no other person on this earth who loves me, God loves me and always will.

A New Thought Pattern

Sometimes I feel lonely and rejected, but God loves me because here's what he did and still does for me:

_____

_____

_____

_____

What will I do today to fix my thoughts more on Jesus and embrace God's truth?

_____

_____

_____

_____

My Prayer

Dear Jesus,

_____

_____

_____

_____

_____

Day Eighteen

The Lie
I don't have a purpose to my life.

I struggle with this lie . . .

| rarely | sometimes | often | all the time |

I struggle to see my purpose in life when . . .

_____

_____

_____

_____

The Bible Says

Set your minds on things above, not on earthly things. For you died, and your life is now hidden with Christ in God. When Christ, who is your life, appears, then you also will appear with him in glory. (Colossians 3:2–4)

Therefore, as God's chosen people, holy and dearly loved, clothe yourselves with compassion, kindness, humility, gentleness and patience. Bear with each other and forgive one another if any of you has a grievance against someone. Forgive as the Lord forgave you. And over all these virtues put on love, which binds them all together in perfect unity. (Colossians 3:12–14)

Let the peace of Christ rule in your hearts, since as members of one body you were called to peace. And be thankful. Let the message of Christ dwell among you richly as you teach and admonish one another with all wisdom through psalms, hymns, and songs from the Spirit, singing to God with gratitude in your hearts. And whatever you do, whether in word or deed, do it all in the name of the Lord Jesus, giving thanks to God the Father through him. (Colossians 3:15–17)

God's Truth

My purpose in life is to love the Lord my God with my heart, soul, and strength and to love others.

A New Thought Pattern

Based on God's truth, here's my new personal mission statement:

_____

_____

_____

_____

What will I do today to fix my thoughts more on Jesus and embrace God's truth?

_____

_____

_____

_____

My Prayer

Dear Jesus,

_____

_____

_____

_____

_____

Day Nineteen

The Lie
I am alone.

I struggle with this lie . . .

rarely   sometimes   often   all the time

This feels very real to me. I don't think it's a lie at all when . . .

_____

_____

_____

_____

_____

The Bible Says

"Be strong and courageous. Do not be afraid or terrified because of them, for the Lord your God goes with you; he will never leave you nor forsake you." (Deuteronomy 31:6)

Turn to me and be gracious to me, for I am lonely and afflicted. Relieve the troubles of my heart and free me from my anguish. (Psalm 25:16,17)

Though my father and mother forsake me, the Lord will receive me. (Psalm 27:10)

"And surely I am with you always, to the very end of the age." (Matthew 28:20)

God has said, "Never will I leave you; never will I forsake you." (Hebrews 13:5)

God's Truth

Even if everyone in my life forsakes me, I am never alone.

A New Thought Pattern

I will try to reach out in these ways to make some personal connections:

_____

_____

_____

Even if my circumstances make it hard to combat loneliness, I can remember this about my Lord and Savior:

_____

_____

_____

What will I do today to fix my thoughts more on Jesus and embrace God's truth?

_____

_____

_____

My Prayer

Dear Jesus,

_____

_____

_____

Day Twenty

The Lie
*I need to be in control of my situation
in order to have value in my life.*

I struggle with this lie . . .

○   ○   ○   ○

rarely   *sometimes*   *often*   *all the time*

I tend to try to control things when . . .

_____

_____

_____

_____

_____

The Bible Says

Therefore if you have any encouragement from being united with Christ, if any comfort from his love, if any common sharing in the Spirit, if any tenderness and compassion, then make my joy complete by being like-minded, having the same love, being one in spirit and of one mind. Do nothing out of selfish ambition or vain conceit. Rather, in humility value others above yourselves, not looking to your own interests but each of you to the interests of the others. In your relationships with one another, have the same mindset as Christ Jesus: Who, being in very nature God, did not consider equality with God something to be used to his own advantage; rather, he made himself nothing by taking the very nature of a servant, being made in human likeness. And being found in appearance as a man, he humbled himself by becoming obedient to death—even death on a cross! (Philippians 2:1-8)

God's Truth

My value is found in Jesus Christ, who humbled himself on a cross to give me value as a child of God.

A New Thought Pattern

When I stop trying to control things but instead let God be my guide, it will change my life in these ways:

_____

_____

_____

What will I do today to fix my thoughts more on Jesus and embrace God's truth?

_____

_____

_____

_____

My Prayer

Dear Jesus,

_____

_____

_____

_____

_____

Day Twenty-One

The Lie
I just can't take it anymore.

I struggle with this lie . . .

○————————○————————○————————○
rarely   sometimes   often   all the time

I feel overwhelmed when . . .

_____

_____

_____

_____

The Bible Says

The Lord is the everlasting God, the Creator of the ends of the earth. He will not grow tired or weary, and his understanding no one can fathom. He gives strength to the weary and increases the power of the weak. Even youths grow tired and weary, and young men stumble and fall; but those who hope in the Lord will renew their strength. They will soar on wings like eagles; they will run and not grow weary, they will walk and not be faint. (Isaiah 40:28–31)

For the Spirit God gave us does not make us timid, but gives us power, love and self-discipline. So do not be ashamed of the testimony about our Lord or of me his prisoner. Rather, join with me in suffering for the gospel, by the power of God. He has saved us and called us to a holy life—not because of anything we have done but because of his own purpose and grace. (2 Timothy 1:7–9)

I can do all this through him who gives me strength. (Philippians 4:13)

God's Truth

I can face whatever I need to face because my God gives me strength.

A New Thought Pattern

When I'm feeling overwhelmed, what can I remind myself about God's strength and whom can I ask for help?

_____

_____

_____

What will I do today to fix my thoughts more on Jesus and embrace God's truth?

_____

_____

_____

My Prayer

Dear Jesus,

_____

_____

_____

_____

_____

Day Twenty-Two

The Lie
*I can't stop feeling guilty
because of what I've done.*

I struggle with this lie . . .

rarely   sometimes   often   all the time

Guilt and shame take over in my life when . . .

_____

_____

_____

_____

The Bible Says

For as high as the heavens are above the earth, so great is his love for those who fear him; as far as the east is from the west, so far has he removed our transgressions from us. (Psalm 103:11,12)

"'Come now, let us settle the matter,' says the LORD. 'Though your sins are like scarlet, they shall be as white as snow; though they are red as crimson, they shall be like wool.'" (Isaiah 1:18)

Therefore, if anyone is in Christ, the new creation has come: The old has gone, the new is here! All this is from God, who reconciled us to himself through Christ. (2 Corinthians 5:17,18)

If we claim to be without sin, we deceive ourselves and the truth is not in us. If we confess our sins, he is faithful and just and will forgive us our sins and purify us from all unrighteousness. (1 John 1:8,9)

God's Truth

My sins have been completely forgiven because of Jesus. I no longer need to feel guilty about anything.

A New Thought Pattern

When guilt tries to take over, I can remind myself of this: Jesus washed all my guilt away. All of it. I can visualize this cleanliness from Jesus in this way:

_____

_____

_____

What will I do today to fix my thoughts more on Jesus and embrace God's truth?

_____

_____

_____

My Prayer

Dear Jesus,

_____

_____

_____

_____

_____

Day Twenty-Three

The Lie
I need to be afraid of all the evil in the world.

I struggle with this lie . . .

rarely   sometimes   often   all the time

These particular evils cause me to be afraid . . .

The Bible Says

"I have told you these things, so that in me you may have peace. In this world you will have trouble. But take heart! I have overcome the world." (John 16:33)

Finally, be strong in the Lord and in his mighty power. Put on the full armor of God, so that you can take your stand against the devil's schemes. For our struggle is not against flesh and blood, but against the rulers, against the authorities, against the powers of this dark world and against the spiritual forces of evil in the heavenly realms. Therefore put on the full armor of God, so that when the day of evil comes, you may be able to stand your ground, and after you have done everything, to stand. Stand firm then, with the belt of truth buckled around your waist, with the breastplate of righteousness in place, and with your feet fitted with the readiness that comes from the gospel of peace. In addition to all this, take up the shield of faith, with which you can extinguish all the flaming arrows of the evil one. Take the helmet of salvation and the sword of the Spirit, which is the word of God. And pray in the Spirit on all occasions with all kinds of prayers and requests. (Ephesians 6:10-18)

God's Truth

Jesus has overcome the evil in the world. He gives me the tools I need to stand firm.

A New Thought Pattern

Read Psalm 27:1: "The LORD is my light and my salvation—whom shall I fear? The LORD is the stronghold of my life—of whom shall I be afraid?" I will remember this when the world seems scary. This is the way I picture God as my stronghold:

What will I do today to fix my thoughts more on Jesus and embrace God's truth?

My Prayer

Dear Jesus,

Day Twenty-four

The Lie
I have no gifts or abilities that God can use.

I struggle with this lie . . .

rarely   sometimes   often   all the time

This lie shows up in my life when . . .

_____

_____

_____

_____

The Bible Says

We have different gifts, according to the grace given to each of us. If your gift is prophesying, then prophesy in accordance with your faith; if it is serving, then serve; if it is teaching, then teach; if it is to encourage, then give encouragement; if it is giving, then give generously; if it is to lead, do it diligently; if it is to show mercy, do it cheerfully. (Romans 12:6–8)

There are different kinds of gifts, but the same Spirit distributes them. There are different kinds of service, but the same Lord. There are different kinds of working, but in all of them and in everyone it is the same God at work. Now to each one the manifestation of the Spirit is given for the common good. To one there is given through the Spirit a message of wisdom, to another a message of knowledge by means of the same Spirit, to another faith by the same Spirit, to another gifts of healing by that one Spirit, to another miraculous powers, to another prophecy, to another distinguishing between spirits, to another speaking in different kinds of tongues, and to still another the interpretation of tongues. All these are the work of one and the same Spirit, and he distributes them to each one, just as he determines. (1 Corinthians 12:4–11)

BIGGER *faith*

God's Truth

The Holy Spirit has gifted me uniquely with one or more spiritual gifts.

A New Thought Pattern

This is a list of three people whom I can ask about the gifts they see in me.

_____

_____

_____

Here's what they said:

_____

_____

_____

What will I do today to fix my thoughts more on Jesus and embrace God's truth?

_____

_____

_____

My Prayer

Dear Jesus,

_____

_____

_____

_____

Day Twenty-five

The Lie
I can accomplish anything I set my mind to.

I struggle with this lie . . .

rarely   sometimes   often   all the time

This lie seems harmless, but so often it leaves me feeling . . .

_____

_____

_____

_____

The Bible Says

But remember the Lᴏʀᴅ your God, for it is he who gives you the ability to produce wealth, and so confirms his covenant, which he swore to your ancestors, as it is today. (Deuteronomy 8:18)

When pride comes, then comes disgrace, but with humility comes wisdom. (Proverbs 11:2)

But, "Let the one who boasts boast in the Lord." For it is not the one who commends himself who is approved, but the one whom the Lord commends. (2 Corinthians 10:17,18)

Now listen, you who say, "Today or tomorrow we will go to this or that city, spend a year there, carry on business and make money." Why, you do not even know what will happen tomorrow. What is your life? You are a mist that appears for a little while and then vanishes. Instead, you ought to say, "If it is the Lord's will, we will live and do this or that." (James 4:13–15)

God's Truth

I want to accomplish anything and everything that aligns with God's will.

A New Thought Pattern

Here is a list of my goals. I will pray over each one as I determine God's will for me.

_____

_____

_____

_____

What will I do today to fix my thoughts more on Jesus and embrace God's truth?

_____

_____

_____

My Prayer

Dear Jesus,

_____

_____

_____

_____

_____

Day Twenty-Six

The Lie
I am a failure.

I struggle with this lie . . .

rarely   sometimes   often   all the time

My mind tends to find the negative when . . .

_____

_____

_____

_____

The Bible Says

For though the righteous fall seven times, they rise again, but the wicked stumble when calamity strikes. (Proverbs 24:16)

Such confidence we have through Christ before God. Not that we are competent in ourselves to claim anything for ourselves, but our competence comes from God. (2 Corinthians 3:4,5)

Not that I have already obtained all this, or have already arrived at my goal, but I press on to take hold of that for which Christ Jesus took hold of me. Brothers and sisters, I do not consider myself yet to have taken hold of it. But one thing I do: Forgetting what is behind and straining toward what is ahead, I press on toward the goal to win the prize for which God has called me heavenward in Christ Jesus. (Philippians 3:12–14)

Let us then approach God's throne of grace with confidence, so that we may receive mercy and find grace to help us in our time of need. (Hebrews 4:16)

BIGGER *faith*

God's Truth

Because of Jesus, I am perfect just the way I am.

A New Thought Pattern

Noticing only my failures is an easy rut to fall into. But here are the positives and blessings that I saw in my day today:

_____

_____

_____

_____

What will I do today to fix my thoughts more on Jesus and embrace God's truth?

_____

_____

_____

_____

My Prayer

Dear Jesus,

_____

_____

_____

_____

_____

Day Twenty-Seven

The Lie
*I don't understand why God lets
bad things happen to good people.*

I struggle with this lie . . .

rarely   sometimes   often   all the time

This lie seems true because I've seen . . .

_____

_____

_____

_____

_____

The Bible Says

But Joseph said to them [his brothers], "Don't be afraid. Am I in the place of God? You intended to harm me, but God intended it for good to accomplish what is now being done, the saving of many lives. So then, don't be afraid. I will provide for you and your children." And he reassured them and spoke kindly to them. (Genesis 50:19-21)

And we know that in all things God works for the good of those who love him, who have been called according to his purpose. (Romans 8:28)

Therefore we do not lose heart. Though outwardly we are wasting away, yet inwardly we are being renewed day by day. For our light and momentary troubles are achieving for us an eternal glory that far outweighs them all. So we fix our eyes not on what is seen, but on what is unseen, since what is seen is temporary, but what is unseen is eternal. (2 Corinthians 4:16-18)

God's Truth

God allows things to happen for a reason. Whether or not I understand his reasons, I know that he is good and loving and has a plan.

A New Thought Pattern

Instead of asking why, I will remember that I am unable to comprehend all that God is and knows. His amazing love means I can be sure of this when I don't understand the bad in our world.

What will I do today to fix my thoughts more on Jesus and embrace God's truth?

My Prayer

Dear Jesus,

Day Twenty-Eight

The Lie
What I think or say isn't important.

I struggle with this lie . . .

rarely   sometimes   often   all the time

I feel this way at home or at work when . . .

_____

_____

_____

_____

The Bible Says

When Esther's words were reported to Mordecai, he sent back this answer: "Do not think that because you are in the king's house you alone of all the Jews will escape. For if you remain silent at this time, relief and deliverance for the Jews will arise from another place, but you and your father's family will perish. And who knows but that you have come to your royal position for such a time as this?" (Esther 4:12–14)

Speak up for those who cannot speak for themselves, for the rights of all who are destitute. Speak up and judge fairly; defend the rights of the poor and needy. (Proverbs 31:8,9)

But in your hearts revere Christ as Lord. Always be prepared to give an answer to everyone who asks you to give the reason for the hope that you have. But do this with gentleness and respect. (1 Peter 3:15)

God's Truth

God gave me a voice to use—to praise him, to bless others, and to proclaim the good news about Jesus.

A New Thought Pattern

God loves to hear my voice when I'm praising him. In what ways can I praise him personally and through my service to others?

_____

_____

_____

What will I do today to fix my thoughts more on Jesus and embrace God's truth?

_____

_____

_____

_____

My Prayer

Dear Jesus,

_____

_____

_____

_____

_____

Day Twenty-Nine

The Lie
My life's situation will never change.

I struggle with this lie . . .

○   ○   ○   ○

rarely   *sometimes*   *often*   *all the time*

Right now I feel stuck because . . .

_____

_____

_____

_____

_____

The Bible Says

The Lord is my shepherd, I lack nothing. He makes me lie down in green pastures, he leads me beside quiet waters, he refreshes my soul. He guides me along the right paths for his name's sake. Even though I walk through the darkest valley, I will fear no evil, for you are with me; your rod and your staff, they comfort me. You prepare a table before me in the presence of my enemies. You anoint my head with oil; my cup overflows. Surely your goodness and love will follow me all the days of my life, and I will dwell in the house of the Lord forever. (Psalm 23:1–6)

Rejoice in the Lord always. I will say it again: Rejoice! Let your gentleness be evident to all. The Lord is near. Do not be anxious about anything, but in every situation, by prayer and petition, with thanksgiving, present your requests to God. And the peace of God, which transcends all understanding, will guard your hearts and your minds in Christ Jesus. (Philippians 4:4–7)

God's Truth

My situation may not change in this life, but God knows my situation. He will help me through it and promises a perfect life in heaven.

A New Thought Pattern

No matter what is going on right now, what has God told me about his presence now and in the future?

_____

_____

_____

What will I do today to fix my thoughts more on Jesus and embrace God's truth?

_____

_____

_____

My Prayer

Dear Jesus,

_____

_____

_____

_____

_____

Day Thirty

The Lie
*I need to perform at a high level
in order to have value in my life.*

I struggle with this lie . . .

○————————————○————————————○————————————○

rarely　　　　　　*sometimes*　　　　　　*often*　　　　　　*all the time*

I especially see myself falling for this lie in these situations . . .

_____

_____

_____

_____

The Bible Says

*Trust in the L*ORD *with all your heart and lean not on your own understanding; in all your ways submit to him, and he will make your paths straight.* (Proverbs 3:5,6)

To some who were confident of their own righteousness and looked down on everyone else, Jesus told this parable: "Two men went up to the temple to pray, one a Pharisee and the other a tax collector. The Pharisee stood by himself and prayed: 'God, I thank you that I am not like other people—robbers, evildoers, adulterers—or even like this tax collector. I fast twice a week and give a tenth of all I get.' But the tax collector stood at a distance. He would not even look up to heaven, but beat his breast and said, 'God, have mercy on me, a sinner.' I tell you that this man, rather than the other, went home justified before God. For all those who exalt themselves will be humbled, and those who humble themselves will be exalted." (Luke 18:9-14)

God's Truth

My value in life is not determined by my performance but by the performance of Jesus—his perfect life and his sacrificial death—for me.

A New Thought Pattern

I'm so thankful that my value in life doesn't depend on me at all, it depends on . . .

_____

_____

_____

_____

What will I do today to fix my thoughts more on Jesus and embrace God's truth?

_____

_____

_____

_____

My Prayer

Dear Jesus,

_____

_____

_____

_____

_____

_____

_____

Conclusion

1. To gain a bigger faith, we need to stop believing the lies of Satan, our culture, and the lies we tell ourselves.

2. To gain a bigger faith, we need to fix our thoughts on Jesus and everything the Bible, God's absolute truth, teaches us.

But you and I both know what sounds simple and straightforward is incredibly challenging. It's a daily struggle not to believe the lies. It's a daily challenge to wrap our lives around God's truth.

So what's been your experience these past 30 days? Has God's truth shined a light on any of the lies you tend to believe? My prayer is that it has.

But let's be real. Gaining a bigger faith by fixing our thoughts on Jesus isn't accomplished after just 30 days or 60 days or 6 months. God's plan for you to gain a bigger faith lasts a lifetime.

**Dear friends, since you have been forewarned,
be on your guard so that you may not be carried away
by the error of the lawless and fall from your secure position.
But grow in the grace and knowledge of our Lord and Savior Jesus Christ.
To him be glory both now and forever! Amen.**
(2 Peter 3:17,18)

God bless you on your journey!

About the Writer

Dr. Bruce Becker currently serves as the executive vice president for Time of Grace. He is also a respected and well-known church consultant, presenter, advisor, podcaster, and author. He has served as lead pastor of two congregations; as a member of several boards; and on many commissions, committees, and task forces. In 2012 he completed his professional doctorate in leadership and ministry management. Bruce and his wife, Linda, live in Jackson, Wisconsin. Find Dr. Becker's podcast, *Bible Threads With Dr. Bruce Becker*, at timeofgrace.org, Apple Podcasts, Spotify, and many other podcasting platforms.

About Time of Grace

Time of Grace is an independent, donor-funded ministry that connects people to God's grace—his love, glory, and power—so they realize the temporary things of life don't satisfy. What brings satisfaction is knowing that because Jesus lived, died, and rose for all of us, we have access to the eternal God—right now and forever.

To discover more, please visit timeofgrace.org or call 800.661.3311.

Help share God's message of grace!

Every gift you give helps Time of Grace reach people around the world with the good news of Jesus. Your generosity and prayer support take the gospel of grace to others through our ministry outreach and help them experience a satisfied life as they see God all around them.

Give today at timeofgrace.org/give or by calling 800.661.3311.

Thank you!